EATING RIGHT WITH MYPLATE

Grains Group

by Megan Borgert-Spaniol

BELLWETHER MEDIA • MINNEAPOLIS, MN

Note to Librarians, Teachers, and Parents:

Blastoff! Readers are carefully developed by literacy experts and combine standards-based content with developmentally appropriate text.

Level 1 provides the most support through repetition of high-frequency words, light text, predictable sentence patterns, and strong visual support.

Level 2 offers early readers a bit more challenge through varied simple sentences, increased text load, and less repetition of high-frequency words.

Level 3 advances early-fluent readers toward fluency through increased text and concept load, less reliance on visuals, longer sentences, and more literary language.

Level 4 builds reading stamina by providing more text per page, increased use of punctuation, greater variation in sentence patterns, and increasingly challenging vocabulary.

Level 5 encourages children to move from "learning to read" to "reading to learn" by providing even more text, varied writing styles, and less familiar topics.

Whichever book is right for your reader, Blastoff! Readers are the perfect books to build confidence and encourage a love of reading that will last a lifetime!

This edition first published in 2012 by Bellwether Media, Inc.

No part of this publication may be reproduced in whole or in part without written permission of the publisher. For information regarding permission, write to Bellwether Media, Inc., Attention: Permissions Department, 5357 Penn Avenue South, Minneapolis, MN 55419.

Library of Congress Cataloging-in-Publication Data
Borgert-Spaniol, Megan, 1989-
 Grains group / by Megan Borgert-Spaniol.
  p. cm. – (Blastoff! readers. Eating right with myplate)
 Summary: "Relevant images match informative text in this introduction to the grains group. Intended for students in kindergarten through third grade"– Provided by publisher.
 Includes bibliographical references and index.
 ISBN 978-1-60014-756-2 (hardcover : alk. paper)
 1. Grain in human nutrition–Juvenile literature. 2. Grain–Juvenile literature. I. Title.
 QP144.G73B67 2012
 641.3'31–dc23   2011033123

Printed in the United States of America, North Mankato, MN.
010112   1207

Contents

The Grains Group

The Grains Group is made up of grains and foods made from grains.

Rice and oats are grains.
Bread and pasta are made
from grains.

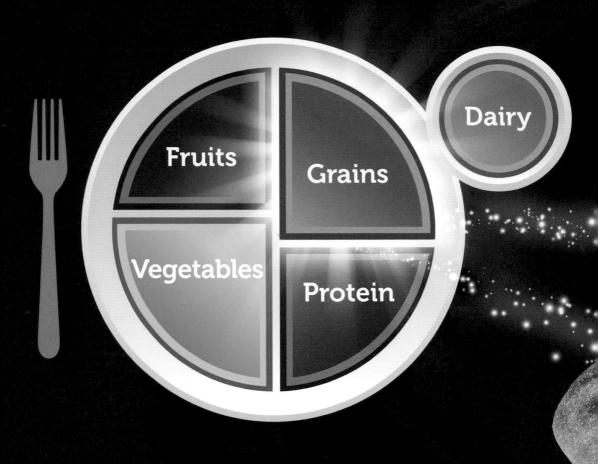

The orange part of **MyPlate**
is the Grains Group.

1 serving = 1 slice of bread
1 small muffin
½ cup cooked rice
½ cup cooked pasta
3 cups popped popcorn

Kids need five servings of grains each day.

Why Are Grains Good For You?

Grains are loaded with **fiber**. Fiber helps move food through your body.

8

Grains are also full of **iron** and **B vitamins**. These give you energy to run and play.

Types of Grains

Half of the grains you eat should be **whole grains**.

Whole grain foods are made
with the entire grain **kernel**.

Brown rice and oatmeal are whole grain foods.

White bread and white rice are not. They do not have as much fiber as whole grain foods.

Eating Grains

Grains fit into every meal. Try whole wheat pancakes in the morning. Add berries to make them sweet.

Top whole grain cereal with fruit for a quick breakfast.

Fill tortillas with rice and beans for lunch.

Choose whole wheat pasta
for spaghetti or macaroni
and cheese.

Oatmeal raisin cookies are a tasty dessert. Make them with whole wheat flour instead of white flour.

Popcorn is another healthy
whole grain snack.

The Grains Group has a whole lot to offer.

Make plenty of room on your plate for foods from this group!

Glossary

B vitamins—parts of some foods that help your body make and use energy

fiber—the part of a plant that stays whole as it moves through your body

iron—a part of some foods that carries oxygen through your blood; this gives you energy.

kernel—the seed of a grain

MyPlate—a guide that shows the kinds and amounts of food you should eat each day

whole grains—grain foods that are made with the entire grain kernel; whole wheat, brown rice, and oatmeal are whole grains.

To Learn More

AT THE LIBRARY

Dolbear, Emily J. *How Did That Get to My Table? Pasta*. Ann Arbor, Mich.: Cherry Lake Pub., 2010.

Hewitt, Sally. *Grains and Cereals*. New York, N.Y.: PowerKids Press, 2008.

Snyder, Inez. *Grains to Bread*. New York, N.Y.: Children's Press, 2005.

ON THE WEB

Learning more about the Grains Group is as easy as 1, 2, 3.

1. Go to www.factsurfer.com.

2. Enter "Grains Group" into the search box.

3. Click the "Surf" button and you will see a list of related Web sites.

With factsurfer.com, finding more information is just a click away.

Index

The images in this book are reproduced through the courtesy of: R. Legosyn, front cover; Morgan Lane Photography, pp. 4-5; U.S. Department of Agriculture, Center for Nutrition Policy and Promotion, p. 6; Juan Martinez, pp. 7, 11, 13, 20; Jordache, pp. 8-9; UpperCut Images / Getty Images, p. 10; Monkey Business Images, p. 12; Sean Justice / Getty Images, p. 14; Leland Bobbe / Getty Images, p. 15; Brett Mulcahy, p. 16; Paul Schiefer Photography / Age Fotostock, p. 17; Shebeko, p. 18; Juerco Boerner / Photolibrary, p. 19; Bipolar / Getty Images, p. 21.